Imagine

Ricky Maeweather

BookLeaf
Publishing

India | USA | UK

Presentation by *BookLeaf Publishing*

Web: www.bookleafpub.com

E-mail: info@bookleafpub.com

ISBN: 9789357214810

First edition 2023

Ruthnie Angrand, Seneca T. Wilson, Words McNeil, Cedric Bolton, Audrey Brown, Michael Gaut, Brandon Powell, Louis Cruz, 210 Teas, The Underground Poetry Spot

ACKNOWLEDGEMENT

Huge thank you to BookLeaf Publishing for making this poetic project come to life!

PREFACE

Sometimes we need a positive or assertive moment to neutralize any negative vibes we may experience, imagining a better outcome achievement helps me push through my path of roadblocks and I hope this book will assist you in doing the same.

We Are Not Candles

The furnace of your future should not be figured out by your friends or family...

You striving, is what sparks the fire...

The length of the wick is determined by your work ethic...

And you never let failure affect your flame...

Burn your way through it, and illuminate every room you enter with influence...

You will send out the scent of success...

Just remember you are important, not a candle...

When The Sun Takes A Break

When you notice the absence of the Sun, don't attempt to search for its existence...

When the sky's appearance matches basement gray floors, and the rain skydives into the ground...

It is the perfect setup for staying in...

Let all of your worries go as you run through your movie list.

Cocoon yourself with your favorite comforter, or cuddle someone you care about...

Move to the notes of your favorite music, like a kite kissing a tornado...

Face the foods that make you fall asleep, with a full stomach of satisfaction...

And let the gloomy day become jealous of the sunshine you create within your window...

Dreams

When your eyelids finally clock out from blinking...

You find yourself sinking into a deep sleep as if the sandman invited you into his castle...

And your body lies still like a compressed flower in your journal...

Your mind may wander into the atmosphere...

And your emotions ignite the images tailored by your thoughts...

Causing you to star as the lead role in the scenarios you create...

Still directing the monologue destined to be remembered when you awake...

Only promote the positive motion pictures...

Nightmares will never sell at the box office...

If Music Was A Woman

Just hearing the sound of your voice makes me vulnerable...

Your beats break down my body...

Your diversity determines my dances...

And your vocals sound like wedding vows...

You pick out the perfect sounds to place into my soul...

I am addicted to your lips and lyrics...

It was love at first song...

I want to massage every music note you manifest...

And spend eternity together within my eardrums...

A Smoothie Recipe For The Soul

This isn't a basic beverage, it should be enriched with your life's essentials...

Start by adding in your personality...

Next, include all of your favorite hobbies...

From there, sprinkle in something special to you.

After that, include a huge amount of achievements...

Make sure you grab a handful of goals to throw in also...

Haters lack substance so just set them aside, they're worthless...

Douse a few dreams on top, and then mix them with your memories...

It should blend into your favorite color, enjoy every sip of success you've created...

Wall Of Words

Someone like you deserves more than the world...

A galaxy of stars doesn't compare to how gorgeous you are...

Spending quality time over conversations hotter than comets...

And if you find a way through my fortress of feelings, prepare for my poet emotions...

Watch as the trust we build up, construct a palace where we will exchange words through our vows...

I will shower you with support, until you are drenched with determination...

Let my love leak out of my veins into your heart, as it pumps throughout your figure of fortune...

Donating my mind, body, and spirit to prove my devotion to you...

I will always be ready and willing to protect
your purity...

You possess the power to erupt roses through the
concrete you walk over...

The gift of switching gray skies to baby blue
with your smile...

Your natural scent relaxes me, like sunsets when
we snuggle...

Your ambition becomes ammunition for my goal
assignments...

I promise to make sure your wedding ring
matches your halo of harmony...

I never tripped over love, but I'm willing to fall
into the future as long as you're with me...

Rise Up

Plant a seed for your success...

It'll work its way through the mulch of mistakes you learn from...

And watch it sprout up from the adversity...

Your potting soil is full of potential...

Number One Fan

Fall in love with everything about yourself...

Support yourself through the great times and struggles...

Admire your own ambition...

Find happiness within your conscience to help eliminate your anxiety...

Your confidence is too pure to be mistaken for cockiness..

Your existence inspires the sun to shine as the world rotates...

Shower in self-love...

High self-esteem opens your pores...

And becomes cleansed by your character...

Smile

What actions do you take when you like
someone?

Do you treasure them with the truth?

Or carry out the crush with curiosity?

I'm handing over a single sheet of paper holding
affection above it...

You're gazing at outlined hearts deciding
whether to check yes or no...

The paper reads...

"So do you like me or not?"

I'm craving an answer as if we were in
kindergarten class together...

Sharing teddy grams...

With two straws...

And one juice box...

Not even caring if I catch cooties...

Nap time dreaming of what we could become...

Finger painting our family on construction
paper...

Glittered with our essence...

Shining in our love...

My picture will never be perfect without you...

A test...

To see if cupid's route to happiness is true...

Selfish enough to neglect the temporaries
waiting for the permanent puzzle piece to your
heart...

Placing patience and time into your portrait.

Ready to frame it with your feelings...

Married to your morals and goals until you reach
the finish line of your future...

You must be tired because you've been running through my mind all day...

Age is nothing but a number when you feel the love will be limitless...

Watching your relationship blossom like blue lotus flowers under the stars...

Floating in orbit...

I can taste the milky way off your lips...

Protective of what fate presented like a mother and her cougar cub...

Witnessing their eyes seeing what you have been waiting and wanting...

Both becoming closer...

Marking your calendar crossing out days until the wedding has been reached...

Both diving off the top of the wedding cake falling into happiness...

Ready to taste the sweet side of being in love as if strawberries never came across your tongue...

You see I want to climb the mountains of your emotions...

I want to swim through the tears falling from your beauty...

I would remove every single rib I have...

Just to make more of you...

So what actions do you take when you like someone?

If I was good with words...

I would express myself through a poem...

Black

My skin is considered a shade...

But no colored signs are what forced us away
back in the day...

Racist-created bands without musical
Instruments by the Klu Klux Clan...

Where they gave my people trees instead of
tickets to hang around for their performance...

We were a fan base of bondage...

Without an option...

My ancestors attended concerts of crucifixions...

Which is why today I refuse to live in a song
written by the sorrow of slaves...

I will never be ashamed of the skin I am in...

Whether you love or hate my complexion you
will respect my melanin...

My culture is submerged in popularity to the
point that others will steal it and deny the
similarity...

My people are innovators...

Far from imitators...

Back home we were Kings and Queens before
the invaders...

We just choose not to wear our crowns today...

But you know our essence is immaculate...
Time freezes from the way we age...

Our race is royalty...

No matter if we dress in black and gold our
black is gold...

They wish they could cause the regression back
to oppression because of our complexion...

Call it a race recession...

It's a master misconception...

But we will never return to that depression...

So cut the cords to the stereotypes...

We are not fried chicken eating...

Grape soda drinking...

Watermelon servants to whomever feels superior
because of our pigment...

The only chains we acknowledge are the chain
of commands from businesses built by us...

Music and sports are not our only options for
passage out of poverty...

We can be doctors, lawyers, presidents...

Our intelligence provides variety....

We're more than a product of our environment...

We are the true trendsetters in society...

Everyone's not a welfare baby some lives have
always been glorious...

And the only "N" word you better call me is
Notorious...

Because I dream big...

Our fashion is unforgettable...

Our dances draw attention...

Our rhythm is natural...

Our hair is rare...

To touch it you need a legit reason...

We're five-star chefs...

All our food gets seasoned...

We're dominant in all that has us determined...

You can give us the shortest month to speak
about our history...

But when it comes down to who actually built
this country that ain't no mystery...

The Declaration never stopped our
assassination...

It wasn't written for us...

We didn't ask to come here that's a simple explanation...

But here were are...

Black and beautiful...

Black and excellent...

Black and Proud...

Black and unapologetic about it...

Our worth is expensive...

Our presence will always be priceless...

And our existence will always...

Matter...

May All Love All

You can mud away others' issues with your motivation...

Change the flat tire of people's problems who's fallen off their road to success...

The fascination of the ocean stems from you flourishing on land unlike the rest of the mermaids...

Never stop being magical...

You have the energy of a unicorn running through the universe...

As a ghost witness you crush your goals...

Your happiness will never have you haunted...

Stargazing into your eyes will inspire...

Hearing the sound of your heartbeat can soothe souls...

Your personality promotes love...

Your aura can be adorable...

You're addicting like tacos....

So never stop building yourself up like one...

My Honest Poem

My name is Ricky Maeweather...

I was born on the 15th of December...

I take pride in being a Sagittarius.

Both bold and blunt, to the point where my heart speaks what my mind struggles to do even when my mouth is sealed shut.

If body language was a martial art, I would be a Grand Master by now.

Trusting my chi to challenge the tasks I take on to achieve in life.

There used to be moments where my spinal cord would abandon me, and I became a paraplegic every time I should have stood up for myself.

There were times where I felt my shadow was the only thing that had my back, whenever my heart went missing.

I was raised by my mother and grandmother,
who both submerged me in sensitivity and
support.

I was given my father's last name, I just wish
more memories came along with it.

My favorite color changed from red to purple.

And my only talent worth talking about included
a pencil and a blank sheet of paper.

To save my mother's money, I would just sketch
my stress away instead of spending it on therapy.

Dreams, taught me how to draw out my
depression.

I chose silverware over sports, and the food
network introduced me to husky clothing for
kids.

I spent the majority of my life hiding inside.

Both my room, and insecurities...

It wasn't until my middle school music teacher
chose me as his lead actor in drama club, that I

realized there was more to life than what society
made its favorites.

I use to always pay the price to be popular,
spending money to be stressed about being
spotted.

Not realizing until later, I could learn to love
being me for free.

I didn't read books but I loved to cook.

Me learning to act, didn't matter that I was fat.

It was about believing in yourself as you
rehearse the pages.

The only time you should feel comfortable being
someone else is performing on stage.

One of my best discoveries is that reality loves
my personality.

My presence can create a positive essence...

I may be insecure, but I know my heart is pure.

I believe we are all built to digress through
anything we endure.

I strive to keep everyone happy around me through my positivity.

Practicing health and wellness, the gym is my sanctuary where I now sweat out stress and solve solutions.

But sometimes, a fat-free bowl of vanilla ice cream is the only thing that can calm my soul.

I live my life logically, and do not believe that anything will last forever.

Which is why I try to manifest every moment into something magical.

I feel love is a drug that many are unable to shake, and sometimes overdose from broken promises and bruises.

So I set up mental marathons and events of emotions, for anyone who feels they can handle what my heart holds.

I love supporting other people's children, I just avoid having my own.

That way I can eliminate the fear of failing them as a father.

I'm a puzzle piece that does not fit in its own family portrait.

So I focus on bettering everyone else's future.

I was brought into this world alone, and logically I'll probably leave the same way.

But sometimes I wish I am wrong...

Painted Picture

If seasons could take photos, you would be
hotter than the summer skies during winter
nights.

Who springs into people's hearts causing them
to fall for you.

You are a vessel unbroken and untouched,
polished with poetry.

With the ability to manufacture memories worth
more than motion pictures.

I guess that makes you the director to our
destiny.

Filled with fields of dandelions and dreams both
crawling to the skies.

Amazed by your organic personality.

Your knowledge is natural,

And you are a masterpiece of imperfections.

Crushing writer's block with your creativity.

A painter's blueprint of the perfect portrait to place into the world's soul.

Each one of your heartbeats gives birth to another relationship in every galaxy.

And if stars had the power to speak, you would gravitate to their center of attention.

They would gossip about your glory.

They would discuss the cuteness of your charisma and conscience.

They would picture themselves polishing your halo and waking up with your wings.

Everything would revolve around you,

Even the sun would become jealous of how hot you are.

Which we both know every day isn't perfect.

And there will be days that your tears will exile themselves from your eyes.

But even in those moments, every drop would splash into something special.

Your tears breathe life into oceans of orchards.

Your tears change deserts into rainforests.

Your tears could cradle Noah's Arc with their streams if they chose to.

Your tears disguise themselves as tidal waves and waterfalls just to flood people's pain away.

And without even noticing it, you've learned to substitute your sadness for strength.

You've learned to trade in your tragedy for triumph.

Which is why there are pyramids built from blocks of your wisdom.

As Pharaohs inhale your fragrance of experience, imagining they have fallen into a sea of commitment and wedding vows.

Causing them to trade in their crown for a camera just to capture that moment worth more than royalty.

And if seasons could take photos, you would be hotter than the summer skies during winter nights.

Who springs into people's hearts causing them to fall for you...

Why I Like Batman

The other day a kid became excited when he noticed the Batman tattoo on my right arm.

He was about six years old and told me that his favorite superhero was Spiderman because he could crawl on walls.

I smiled, and I told him that I think he's cool also.

He then asked, what made me like Batman?

I never really thought about it until then.

I realized, me and Batman are not that different from each other.

Besides him losing both his parents at a young age growing up to being a billionaire.

The rest of the story I can relate to.

I mean his suit's black and I'm black.

He has a bat signal, I have a cell phone service.

And I'm pretty sure the wall built to protect my feelings is just as strong as his body armour.

If not, then it's stronger.

You see Batman fights crime.

And I'm just trying to fight the fake.

But what do you do when your own friends and family are the villains?

It doesn't take the world's greatest detective to realize when you're being used and lied to.

Abused by the ones you cried to.

So what's the point of caring for a family tree if it grows nothing but Poison Ivy?

And then some wonder why people's hearts beat cold like Mr.Freeze as if their loss of loyalty didn't just drop the temperature below zero.

Robin you for your kindness.

Oh, and my favorite line I hear from people who had problems with me in the past is.

"I'm sorry, I just didn't understand you."

As if I'm some type of complicated riddle that no one can figure out.

So they choose to assume the worst.

But unlike The Riddler, if you just came to me and asked, I would've given you the answer.

But what's the point of figuring it out if you don't even trust me?

As if getting to know me is a combination lock without the numbers.

But if you were a true friend from the start.

You would already have the skills of a locksmith so don't even bother wasting either one of our time.

And just like the Joker I find myself laughing at my life.

Like how Batman's father isn't alive for his birthdays.

And my dad just forgets about mine.

I wonder if Batman uses his cape to wipe the tears away.

No because Batman wouldn't cry so why should I?

I mean, heroes are created to save, not sob.

And to seek justice is their job.

So why would Batman worry about my personal problems versus a bank being robbed?

But we all know life isn't perfect so it really doesn't bother me.

And sometimes money isn't worth more than an apology.

Unless you pay bills...

So I understand why Bruce Wayne fights crime to escape the pain.

And if pieces of my heart were ripped into the shape of bats I would do the same.

Just so others wouldn't have to suffer from the truth that sometimes the bad guys are sitting right inside of your circle.

Smiling, with their two-faced personality right in front of you deciding which knife would make the perfect incision into your spine.

Now I see why Batman chooses to shed light on The Dark Knight.

And I also know the feeling of being alone in times of need finding myself trapped in a Batcave inhaling stress with no exit.

Just to realize that you can't always count on someone rushing to your rescue.

So you learn to become your own superhero.

So when this six-year-old kid asked me why I liked Batman.

I told him...

Because he's way cooler than Spiderman.

Roses

I was told that roses are red.

But my roses are chocolate.

Far from a candy-coated floral creation.

This sweet sleeve of a masterpiece is tattooed on me.

Each petal, planted in its proper place.

No vines green of envy are allowed any space.

These Hershey kissed buds on my skin were meant to blossom into the same love and hate.

From the seeds of people I've learned lessons from.

More than just a Valentine's Day cliche.

These bushes of beauty represent the people I've lost.

The people I love...

And the few I never even cared about.

We buy these bundles of beauty in stores not
really taking the time out to understand.

What placed them in that position?

Who decides on which roses stay in the fields as
the others go on sale?

Not knowing what it took just to reach the point
of being picked out for an occasion.

Not realizing that each one of those seeds grew a
different type of story through its very own soil.

Not every rose may have been kept up and cared
for.

Not every rose may have been fertilized and
fashioned to society's liking.

I'm sure there are roses every day that don't
make the cut just because of the color they chose
to blossom into.

Refusing to grow like the rest of the bunch.

Embracing the adversity and still sprouting through the sand.

Far too focused and strong to let the stress take over from the rain that never arrives.

Learning to trust and believe in the things they strive for every day.

Understanding that even when the sun turns its back on them.

There is a bright side somewhere waiting to be discovered.

Realizing that every leaf that sprouts, will not make it to the floral finish line.

There are weeds disguised throughout your life that will attempt to stunt your growth.

Weeds, secretly soiled with lies and watered by betrayal.

Attempting to hold you down beside them in their field of failure.

Jealous, of seeing you start from the very bottom of the ground.

And witnessing you bloom into a bright future.

We just use their fear as fertilizer.

And through every rosebud, there is a battle.

Many of us are captured by their attraction.

But how many of you felt the same thorns they
went through?

How many of you were pricked into shedding
the same color that stains each petal you adore?

Scattered over your bed and floor during that
romantic night?

We sometimes forget what looks so delightful,
can also be dangerous.

Just like how a simple smile can distract the rest
from your true stress.

A rose can be the perfect representation of love
in a wedding.

Then turn around and be the proper pick for a
loss in a casket.

I guess it's okay to say that they were made to be a love or hate bouquet.

But before the sun, follows the rain.

And even the most beautiful rose has thorns that can cause pain.

But every day we choose to live.

Is another opportunity to increase our intelligence.

To value ourselves and love diversity.

Constantly learning from life or university.

We were not created just to settle and sustain pain.

Unlike these roses, we have the right to fight for what we believe in.

We were not born to be enslaved and shown off for others' appreciation.

We have a choice, to speak our mind louder than waterfalls dancing with tsunamis.

Spread the love like wildfires.

And let everything it touches burn with affection.

Hatred only causes things to rot.

We do not depend on the sun to determine our destiny.

We do not wait for the rain to shower our stress away.

We only see the ground as a memory from where we first started up.

You were born to build your own life.

Be bold!

Be brave!

And never stop believing in yourself!

So plant a seed into your heart.

And watch it grow from everything you've placed your time into.

Roses usually come in a dozen, but your dreams should always be limitless.

I wear these roses to remind me of how my life's been.

There are lessons in these leaves.

And every time I stare at them.

They show me I still have more growing up to do.

Pay Attention

Pay attention...

You were placed in a pool of prosperity with the option to either swim,

or sink...

This is the time where you decide to keep it real or actually think.

Walking the wrong road could lead you into a coffin and I'm coughing.

Because I am sick,

I am sick of the consequences you sustain because you refuse to use your brain.

Lacking respect for yourself causing your loved ones pain I mean it's insane!

Even your tongue speaks ignorance when you try to explain!

The moves you make the risk you take for popularity's sake?

You're sleepwalking with the wrong intentions when you should be awake.

Who, are you living for?

Too busy being a follower what would you do if destiny knocked on your door?

But you would never know if dreams came knocking cause you are never home.

You front like you're a spartan cause the block is where you roam.

Listen I'm grown...

I became a bank to these streets and I left it alone.

You think it's cute to play the blocks and carry glocks just to sell rocks?

It all seems fun until you're introduced to someone else's gun.

There's no name on the bullet when they pull it.

It goes from guns to aggression leading to funerals and depression.

They lose their life you lose your freedom now your future's in question.

Probably over money and drugs in this recession.

So take notes you will need them class is in session...

Your conscience is yelling inside...

That's the regression...

You better pray your trial make it in heaven.

Just imagine who fell into hell...

That's the real life lesson...

As I search for explanations of the younger generations.

Kids strive for play stations more than education.

We need to clean up their act I'm callin
sanitation because I am tired of waitin...

It seems as if we experience violence more than
on vacation.

You see I am a poetic descendant here to show
the dependents the meaning of Independence.

So that the chosen ones who experience
parenthood will love it instead of living it like a
sentence.

These babies did not ask you to bring them into
this world so add love and protection subtract
the neglection.

Raising kids isn't cheap but what's free is the
affection.

Correction, is the facility they use to mold your
ability.

To do good whether you're raised in the suburbs
or hood I know it's tough living misunderstood.

Which is why we need to infiltrate our mind
with small incisions of smart decisions to value
our positive intentions.

Listen...

Our thoughts we currently fail to mention can be
this era's greatest invention.

But it all starts by paying attention.

Butterflies Don't Have A Finish Line

Previously a caterpillar of poverty...

Inspired inch by inch...

Motivated by its movement...

Unlike bees waiting for their pollen promotion.

They resign from the cacoon created within to start their career...

Ready to fly into its future...

You may be blinded by their beauty...

But they're more focused on the workload they can carry onto their wings...

Reflection

When I look into a mirror...

The image staring back at me doesn't seem happy...

My reflection has the audacity to show I am not the best version of me...

As if this lifeless object is certified in therapy...

The nerve...

To think I'm not trying to be different than the rest...

And continue doing my best...

My potential is somewhere under this laziness...

I just need the motivation to clean up this mess...

We often find ourselves drowning in doubt...

Lacking the energy to see what our talents are actually about...

Instead of living we are just existing...

Waking up to pay bills and apply to a job
listing...

Being an adult can be sickening...

We were not placed on this earth to live beneath
our worth...

At least have aspirations of vacations...

My reflection was giving me direction...

Not to suffer from the assumptions of others...

Never bite your tongue when being disrespected
by anyone old or young...

Don't let low self-esteem negate you from
chasing your dream...

If you want success you have to see it through...

You'd be surprised by who actually supports you
too...

It's usually the unexpected who believes in
you...

You just have to believe in yourself...

And stop letting your goals sit and collect dust
on your insecurity shelf...

If you strive for satisfaction you need to be
about that action...

Hesitation will never lead you to your
destination...

It's okay to feel inspiration from your
imagination...

Let your confidence be your compass to your
accomplishments and celebration...

Be the farmer of your future...

Enjoy the fruits of your labor from the
manifestation...

Your dedication is medication...

You don't have to be a doctor...

But you need to have patience...

Sometimes our motivation just needs
maintenance...

You may not always correct every
imperfection...

But the first step in making any positive change
is by looking into your reflection...

Try

Use love to lift them out when sinking in their own quicksand of stress...

Become better than their shadow through their light and dark times...

Make them feel you're their favorite dessert helping destroy depression...

Sweet support may substitute the sadness...

Remind them how valuable their worth and crown is when their confidence becomes crooked...

White Dress

I always dream of the woman I want, but I never search for her when I awake...

Her beauty leaves kisses on the canvas leading to my attraction...

And now my eyes are catching flames because I always forget to blink when I'm in her presence...

There may be plenty of fish in the sea but they aren't worth what this miracle mermaid has to offer...

So I guess you can say she's been swimming through my mind non stop and I'm drowning from the desire I have for her...

Slowly sinking...

Not gasping for air but gasping for courage to surf the waves all the way to her heart through this sea of commitment...

I can tell she's selfish with her sex appeal...

Giving me an addiction for sleeping pills and
nNyQuil just to spend more time with her...

And not once have I ever come across the right
letters on my tongue just to tell her...

"I like you"

I never met someone with so much class to make
me constantly fail her course just to continue to
learn from her...

Until she feels I am ready for our future...

Studying the art of honesty and faithfulness for
this final of happiness...

Graduating from a boy to a man...

Making my diploma melt into that wedding ring
I pictured the night our eyes danced together for
the first time...

Cupid played her favorite song...

Throwing my scholarships in the air as they
cuddle with the sky as doves.

Falling into the ground as rose petals...
And my cap and gown blossom into the tuxedo
our future picked out for us.

Just like the flower placed in her hair...

As she walks out of my dream down that aisle
into my heart...

In her white dress...

My Neighborhood Garden

My personality was planted in the garden of my
neighborhood...

I blossom...

Every morning the sun stretches in front of me.

As parks breathe life into my bones...

I grow tall from the rays of kids' smiles...

Fertilized by diverse cultures...

I am cultivated by the community...

With visions witnessing the area's attraction...

Not even the future can look past these buildings
as if beauty swallowed their brick bodies...

And the only races children judge are from one
light post to the next...

As if Olympic gold medals learned how to run
on rose petals...

And our hairstyles inform us of neighborhood
news before the media even airs it...

All because we build barbershops and salons
with loud voices...

Flirting with the ambiance...

While the streets painting the perfect picture...

We must've hired cover girls as construction
workers...

I watch little kids grow wings in corner stores
spending their grandparents' change feeling they
are in candyland heaven...

A sweet tooth never shined so bright...

As they ignore the airheads afraid of catching
cavities...

I watch them stare down the sweet aisle going
nuts with almond joy drunk off the happiness of
a Hershey Bar.

It must have been payday...

As we watch these starburst into success raising
them to reach past the stars onto the milky way
just to show the world what comes from our
candy shop community.

It's sweet dreams and memories...

Wake up and realize where you grew up and
what printed the perfect resume for life's
interview...

Promote yourself with pride and celebrate...

Home is where the heart is and cold shoulders
are never welcomed to this house party.

I watch schools graduate my neighbors into
life-size degrees making destiny request their
hand in marriage...

You see,

Unity wasn't born with a race...

And support never came with a complexion...

Everyday we awake with fins just to dance
through this amazing ocean named diversity...

Where we mix our heritage together into the
perfect clay to mold what will inspire our
dreams into reality taped film ready to project...

A movie that'll always be in the making...

With one mind...

One breathe...

And one heartbeat...

So if want to witness where I was raised...

Make sure you get your ticket...

I was planted in the garden of my
neighborhood...

And I grew up...

To be a role model...

9 789357 214810